WAT TAKES HIS SHOT

*The Life & Legacy
of Basketball Hero
Wataru Misaka*

by **Cheryl Kim**
illustrated by **Nat Iwata**

LEE & LOW BOOKS INC.
New York

Wataru Misaka entered the world as a ball of energy! Living in a tight space beneath his father's barbershop, Wat found creative ways to keep moving. His family couldn't afford expensive sports equipment, but that didn't stop Wat. He built his own high jump using bamboo poles and a dirt pile. Wat always found a way to overcome a challenge.

Every Sunday in Ogden, Utah, Wat raced to the park. He loved playing basketball with first-generation Issei like his parents, second-generation Nisei like himself, and third-generation Sansei. Since they were not allowed to join the whites-only sports leagues, the Japanese American community formed their own.

Wat dribbled with speed and took his shots. Yet, he shared the ball as much as he scored. Wat loved being part of a team.

As Wat spent more time on the court, his passion for the game grew. In the evenings, Wat shot baskets into the dimly lit net near his school. When he missed, his father would tell him, "Gambatte. Do your best."

GAMBATTE

Wat shot again and again, night after night, until he barely missed at all.

In junior high, Wat joined his school's basketball team. His coach and classmates noticed his skills. After helping his team win the city tournament, Wat knew he could hold his own on the court.

Some of Wat's high school teammates towered over him, but Wat didn't mind. He darted and whizzed around his opponents, leading his team to their first state championship.

The seasons changed and a few months after Wat turned fifteen, his father passed away. Wat's mother worried how she would provide for him and his two younger brothers.

"We should move back to Japan," she suggested.

"What about basketball? My team?" Wat asked.

"I can't support our family on my own," she said.

"I'll help out! I'll get a job," Wat promised.

Wat's mother agreed to stay, and Wat helped to take care of her and his siblings. He worked hard at school, on the court, and on his cousin's farm to support his family.

On December 7, 1941, the radio blared, "Japanese attack on Pearl Harbor!" Japan's military had bombed a US naval base in Hawaii. The next day, the US declared war on Japan and entered World War II. Wat's heart felt sick. The country his parents called home and the country he called home were fighting against each other.

The US government feared an attack on the West Coast. That fear, fueled by racism, led many to believe that Japanese Americans living in the US were enemies. President Franklin D. Roosevelt signed an executive order that forced nearly 122,000 Issei, Nisei, and Sansei in California, Washington, Oregon, and Arizona to move into incarceration camps. They were not given their right to a fair trial and lost their houses and treasured possessions, their businesses, their freedom—everything.

Since Wat and his family lived in Utah, they were allowed to stay in their home. The government moved more than 11,000 Japanese Americans to the Topaz War Relocation Center in Wat's home state. The majority of those in the Utah camp were Nisei, born in America, just like Wat.

Wat knew he needed to continue his education while he still had his freedom. Going to college would help him get a job to continue supporting his family.

In 1943, university dorms in Utah were segregated. Wat was told there were no more dorm rooms available for him, so he slept under the bleachers in the gym. One morning, he spotted a poster on the gym door. Basketball tryouts! Wat wrestled with the idea of playing basketball again. *I'm here to earn an engineering degree, not a spot on a team.*

Gambatte! his father would say. *Do your best.* Wat knew he did his best with a ball in his hand. He showed up for tryouts. Although he was the shortest player, he made the first cut, the second cut, and the third. Wat was officially a college basketball player.

"YOU DON'T BELONG HERE!"

Despite Wat's skills, he and a fellow Nisei teammate, Masateru
"Tut" Tatsuno, spent most games on the bench. When Wat did
play, angry voices hounded him from the sidelines.
For the first time on a court, Wat felt like an outsider.

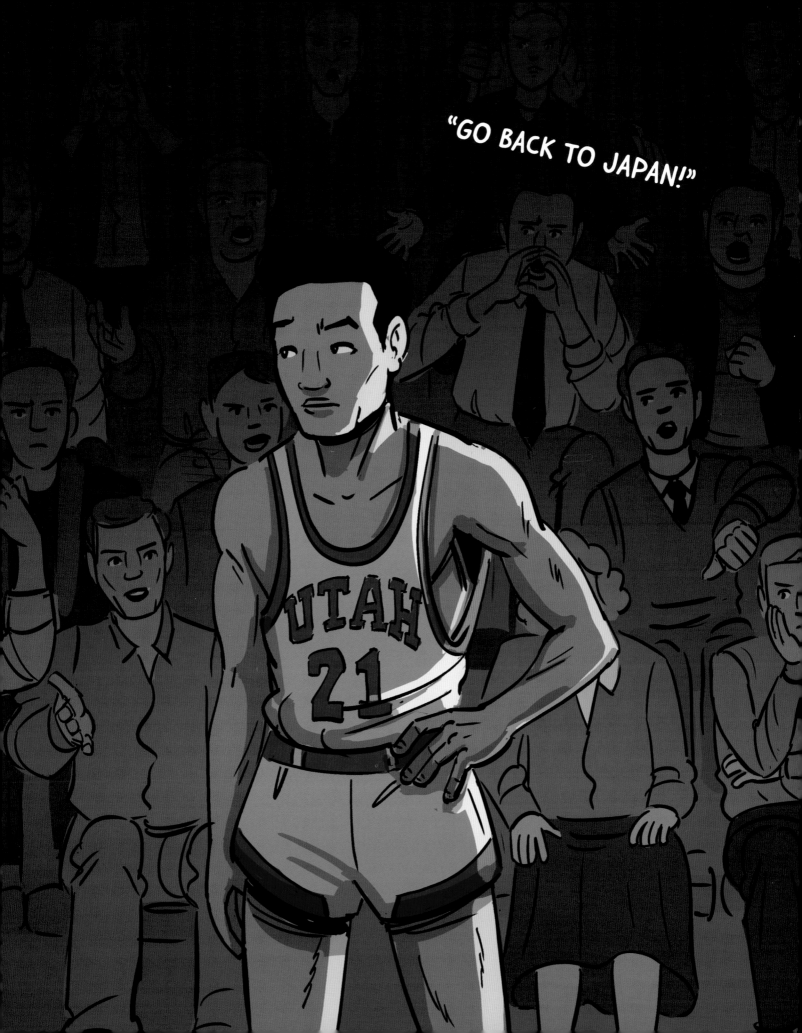

Before the final game of the year, a starting teammate got hurt and Wat took his place. *I'll show you what I can do*, he thought.

GAMBATTE

The louder the crowd yelled insults, the faster Wat ran. The more they waved their fists at him, the more aggressively he drove to the basket. He swiped, passed, leaped . . . and sank three baskets. Wat's team took the lead!

"He's the fastest man I've seen on the court!" said the announcer.

With seconds left, Wat sent a high-arcing floater . . . *SWISH*.

They were champions!

In honor of their team's big win, Wat and his teammates received personalized championship blankets. Tut didn't go to the final game, so Wat accepted Tut's blanket on his behalf. Wat had an idea to surprise Tut with it.

Wat went with Tut to visit the Topaz camp, where Tut's family was being held. Barracks made of pine planks and tar paper sat in rows atop dry, cracked land. The camp looked like a prison.

Wat presented the blanket to Tut in front of his family. They proudly draped it over the wood-framed bunker.

Both young and old began to gather.

"We listened to every game!" one child told them.

"You're heroes!" said another.

Wat looked at the smiling faces and realized he and Tut were more than champions. By bringing their best to each game, they brought hope to an entire community.

The next basketball season, Wat and other teammates were drafted into the US military. Wat joined other Nisei in the Military Intelligence Service Language School. He spent ten hours a day learning how to read, write, and speak Japanese fluently. Wat became a staff sergeant.

On August 6 and August 9, 1945, the United States dropped atomic bombs on the Japanese cities Hiroshima and Nagasaki. More than 200,000 civilians lost their lives on those days. Although the war officially ended six days after the bombings, Wat was sent to Hiroshima, where he interviewed survivors and listened to their stories. He would never forget the devastation he saw. With a heavy heart, Wat returned to Utah to finish his degree.

World War II was in the past but anti-Japanese feelings were still present when Wat returned home. Wat wasn't sure if he'd be given another chance to play basketball. He did not receive the same welcome home as did his white teammates who also served in the war. They returned to their spots on the team while Wat would have to try out again with the new students. *Was it worth it?*

Wat knew he'd face opposition, but he also knew he could contribute. There'd be more critics, but he remembered his Japanese American community cheering for him. Furious spectators might tell him to "go home," but he knew home was here.

Wat blocked the doubts. He loved the game. At tryouts, he fought his way through the first cut, the second cut, and the third to get back on the team.

With World War II fresh on everyone's minds, Wat's coach didn't think he should play at away games. Wat watched as the rest of his teammates packed their bags—on the court or off, he still wasn't one of them.

If they would just give me a chance, I could show them I belong here. We belong here.

During a home game, two teammates were injured.

"Wat!" yelled his coach. "You're in."

Wat jumped to his feet.

He dashed all over the court, stole the ball, made perfect passes, and scored the winning point. No one could deny Wat was the star of the game. From then on, Wat played as a starter and joined the traveling team. Game after game, Wat continued to impress and inspire.

At the end of the season, Wat stepped into Madison Square Garden for the national championship. His team was set to play the Kentucky Wildcats, the defending champions and the number-one team in college basketball. Their superstar, Ralph Beard, was known as the best, fastest, top-scoring player in the country.

Wat's mission was to block Ralph. *Gambatte!* thought Wat. *Just do my best. For my team. For my community.*

As soon as the game began, Wat launched into full speed. With
laser focus, he hustled, swiped, and stayed one step in front of Ralph.
By the second half, Wat's relentless defense sent Ralph to the bench.

As the buzzer went off, Wat pumped his fist in the air! His teammates surrounded him. Utah won 49–45. The crowd leaped to their feet, cheering for *him*, a Japanese American.

Back home, the entire town of Ogden celebrated the win. Wat stood tall as he pictured his family and all the Issei, Nisei, and Sansei who rooted for him all along. But they weren't the only ones who recognized his talent . . .

In 1947, the New York Knicks picked Wat to join their team. Thrilled to continue playing the game he loved, Wat signed the contract. He became the first non-white player in history to join the Basketball Association of America (BAA). The BAA later became the National Basketball Association (NBA).

Wat played three games and scored seven points with the Knicks. When the Knicks released Wat from his contract because they had too many point guards, the Harlem Globetrotters' exhibition basketball team offered Wat a spot. Instead of joining them, Wat decided to return to school to finish his engineering degree.

Wat became an engineer. Even in the corporate world, he was recognized for excellence in team leadership.

Wat stayed active backpacking, bowling, golfing, and serving in his community. He joined an advisory board for youth counseling and started a bowling league for Japanese Americans.

Wat's groundbreaking achievement in professional basketball paved the way for more Asian American players, like Raymond Townsend and Rex Walters, who were both first-round NBA draft picks. When a new generation of fans cheered for Jeremy Lin, so did Wat. The two met and exchanged jerseys.

As Wat and Jeremy shook hands, they were more than just great ballplayers—they were hoopsters of hope, for the young and old, the short and tall, and all who just want their shot.

Author's Note

I remember when "Linsanity" made headlines in the NBA and the pride our family felt to see an Asian American athlete breaking stereotypes. It led me to discover that the first person to break racial barriers in professional basketball was a man named Wataru Misaka. I wondered why I hadn't heard of him.

As I began to research his life, what struck me about Wataru was not only what he had accomplished, but the time period in which he accomplished it. At a time when Japanese Americans were being imprisoned and treated unjustly, what was *his* inspiration and motivation to keep going? I knew that to write this story, I first had to reach out to Wat himself.

Wataru Misaka, 2008

Even at the age of ninety-three, Wat was willing to share his experiences with me and read an early version of the manuscript. He attributed his persistence and can-do attitude to being raised with the Japanese tradition of *gambatte*. In English, it can translate into "do your best" or "hang in there!" and there are different forms and usages of the word when spoken. The more formal and polite usage is "Gambatte, kudasai" or "Please try your best." Gambatte was his life's motto.

Wat was seventeen when nearly 122,000 Japanese Americans with at least "one drop of Japanese blood" living along the West Coast were forced to move into government incarceration camps. They lost everything and were imprisoned for four years with a lack of food, medical care, and basic privacy.

Wat's teammate Masateru "Tut" Tatsuno, from California, was one of about 4,000 students who avoided incarceration because they were granted special permission to attend a university, as long as it was not on the West Coast. This opportunity was the result of work done by the National Japanese American Student Relocation Council. Tut's brother, Dave Tatsuno, lived in the Topaz Relocation Center and smuggled his camera inside. He secretly recorded everyday life in the community, including the interaction between Wat and Tut during their visit. From birthday parties to religious services, his rare footage captured ordinary moments in dire conditions.

Within the confinements of the incarceration camps, Japanese Americans came together to design and build sports fields and courts, organize Girl and Boy Scouts, create art and music schools, plant gardens, form volunteer groups, and so much more. They created hope from a place of despair and formed a community within a place of desolation.

After visiting the Topaz Relocation Center, Wat said he felt immense gratitude for the opportunities and chances he was given. He didn't take anything for granted. Wat also said, "It was a real strange experience to be free—not from prejudice, but free—and playing the game I loved in my home state, while others were being treated like criminals."

While Wat spoke some Japanese, he would later learn the language in the Military Intelligence Service Language School. He was sent to Japan a few months after the bombings to interview survivors. While there, he met an uncle for the first time. His uncle's home barely escaped the blast, but Wat witnessed the complete and utter destruction caused by the bomb. Over the next few months, thousands more died from burns and radiation sickness. Wat returned from Hiroshima with a heavy heart. "I was a man without a country," Wat said. "To the Japanese, I was an invader. Americans didn't trust me because I was Japanese."

Wat disagreed with how the US government ended the war, but he still considered the United States his home. He also knew he couldn't change the past but could only move forward. Despite enduring racism, he fought for his right to play the game he loved.

Even when Wat's basketball career ended, he continued to live an active life, championing for his community and the next generation. He served on several boards, was president of the Japanese American Citizens bowling league for twenty years, and was a member of the Japanese Church of Christ. Even in his nineties, he backpacked into the Wind River Range (Rocky Mountains) every year, golfed once a week, and bowled twice a week.

My hope is that this story encourages young readers—especially those who feel marginalized or whose value feels diminished due to race, abilities, or other differences—to continue taking their shots. Racism, rejection, and exclusion are very real issues that continue to impact our world. Yet, in the midst of it all, persistence, an enduring spirit, and triumph can grow from adversity. Like Wat, we can still choose to bounce back from the challenges and pursue resilience.

"Gambatte—persistence, triumph over adversity, enduring spirit, resilience . . . guided much of my effort and attitude."

—Wataru Misaka

"As I look back on the honors Wat has been given, many allude to his team spirit and his effort to do his best to make the team succeed rather than gain personal glory."

—Katie Misaka (Wat Misaka's wife), former teacher and librarian

Author's Sources

Austin, Allan. *From Concentration Camp to Campus: Japanese American Students and World War II.* Champaign, Illinois, University of Illinois Press, 2007.

Block, Justin. "The Complete History of Asian American Players in the NBA." *Complex*, September 12, 2013.

Custer, Joe J. "Utah's Cinderella Kids Take National NCAA Title in Overtime in New York Garden." *The Ogden Standard Examiner*, March 29, 1944.

Fox, Margalit. "Dave Tatsuno, 92, Whose Home Movies Captured History, Dies." *New York Times*, February 13, 2006.

Frank, Joel S. *Asian American Basketball: A Century of Sport, Community and Culture.* Jefferson, NC: McFarland, 2016.

Hernandez, Rocio. "Japanese American Former Basketball Star Inspired On and Off the Court." *NPR*, November 23, 2019.

Houston, Jeanne Wakatsuki., and James D. Houston. *Farewell to Manzanar: A True Story of Japanese American Experience during and after the World War II Internment.* New York: Ember, 2012.

Johnson, Bruce Alan, dir., and Christine Toy Johnson, prod. *Transcending: The Wat Misaka Story.* DVD. Filmmakers Library, 2011.

Misaka, Wataru. Personal resume. May 30, 2017.

Misaka, Wataru, and Katie Misaka. Personal email interview. May 26, 2017.

Odeven, Ed. "Hoop Pioneer Wat Misaka Reflects on Breaking Barriers in an Incredible Life." *The Japan Times*, December 28, 2019.

"Ouster of All Japs in California Near." *San Francisco Examiner*, February 27, 1942.

Regalado, Samuel. "Sport and Community in California's Japanese-American Yamato Colony." *Journal of Sport History* 19, no. 2 (1992): 12–13.

Stanford Medicine Ethnogeriatrics. "Terminology." Accessed March 14, 2022, https://geriatrics.stanford.edu/ethnomed/japanese/introduction/terminology.html.

Stanley, Jerry. *I Am an American: A True Story of Japanese Internment.* New York, Crown for Young Readers, 1996.

Tatsuno, Dave. "Tut Tatsuno Visits from University of Utah." Uploaded by Nikkei Album, August 23, 2012, http://www.discovernikkei.org/en/nikkeialbum/items/3597/.

The University of Utah Continuum. "That's Just How It Was." Accessed March 30, 2017, https://continuum.utah.edu/departments/thats-just-how-it-was/.

"Utah World War II Stories: VICTORY!" PBS Utah. PBS Utah Production. Accessed August 2020, https://www.pbsutah.org/pbs-utah-productions/shows/utah-world-war-ii-stories/victory/.

"Video from the Topaz, Utah, Japanese Internment Camp during WWII." YouTube, uploaded by *The Salt Lake Tribune*, September 8, 2012.

Walters, James E. "Underdog Westerners Score 49–45 Triumph." *Logansport Pharos-Tribune*, March 25, 1947.

"Wat Misaka 2011 JACL Award Video and Acceptance Speech." YouTube, uploaded by Bruce Alan Johnson, November 12, 2012.

For Nathanael, Zachary, Elijah, and Micah —C. K.

*To my father, Mitsuo, who taught me to work hard,
choose my words thoughtfully, and be myself* —N. I.

Acknowledgments

Thank you to Wataru and Katie Misaka for helping us share this story; my editor, Kandace Coston, for championing Wat's story; critique partners Andrea J. Loney, Suzanne Poulter Harris, and Frances Kalavritinos; my writing community SCBWI Norcal, 12 x 12; agent Jennifer March Soloway; readers Debbie Ridpath Ohi, Mia Wenjen, Kristine Kuwano, Emi Alicaya, and Loretta Ashizawa. Last, but not least, my parents, Peter and Sue Tow; my husband, Brandon; Char and Cam; Jen, Joy, Hope, Zoe, April; and friends for your ongoing inspiration and support.

Photos courtesy of "Transcending—the Wat Misaka Story"

LEE & LOW BOOKS INC., 95 Madison Avenue, New York, NY 10016
leeandlow.com

Edited by Kandace Coston
Book design by Christy Hale
Book production by The Kids at Our House
The text is set in Lexia.
The illustrations are rendered digitally.
Manufactured in China by Toppan

1 3 5 7 9 10 8 6 4 2
First Edition

Library of Congress Cataloging-in-Publication Data
Names: Kim, Cheryl, author. | Iwata, Nat, illustrator.
Title: Wat takes his shot : the life & legacy of basketball hero Wataru Misaka /
by Cheryl Kim ; illustrated by Nat Iwata. Description: First edition. | New York, N.Y. :
Lee & Low Books Inc., [2024] | Includes bibliographical references. | Audience: Ages 6–12 |
Summary: "The biography of Japanese American basketball star Wataru Misaka,
the first person of color to play for the National Basketball Association"—Provided by publisher.
Identifiers: LCCN 2023024678 | ISBN 9781643796031 (hardcover) | ISBN 9781643797144 (ebk)
Subjects: LCSH: Misaka, Wat,—Juvenile literature. | Basketball players—United
States—Biography—Juvenile literature. | Japanese Americans—Biography—Juvenile literature.
Classification: LCC GV884.M56 K56 2024 | DDC 796.323092
[B]—dc23/eng/20230731
LC record available at https://lccn.loc.gov/2023024678